W0113945

Helen Keller

THIS EDITION

Produced for DK by WonderLab Group LLC
Jennifer Emmett, Erica Green, Kate Hale, *Founders*

Editor Maya Myers; **Photography Editor** Kelley Miller; **Managing Editor** Rachel Houghton;
Designers Project Design Company; **Researcher** Michelle Harris; **Copy Editor** Lori Merritt;
Indexer Connie Binder; **Proofreader** Susan K. Hom; **Sensitivity Reader** Ebonye Gussine Wilkins
Series Reading Specialist Dr. Jennifer Albro

First American Edition, 2025
Published in the United States by DK Publishing, a division of Penguin Random House LLC
1745 Broadway, 20th Floor, New York, NY 10019

Copyright © 2025 Dorling Kindersley Limited
24 25 26 27 10 9 8 7 6 5 4 3 2 1
001-345876-May/2025

All rights reserved.
Without limiting the rights under the copyright reserved above, no part of this publication may be reproduced, stored in or introduced
into a retrieval system, or transmitted, in any form, or by any means (electronic, mechanical, photocopying, recording, or otherwise),
without the prior written permission of the copyright owner.
Published in Great Britain by Dorling Kindersley Limited

A catalog record for this book is available from the Library of Congress.
HC ISBN: 978-0-5939-6633-4
PB ISBN: 978-0-5939-6632-7

DK books are available at special discounts when purchased in bulk for sales promotions, premiums, fund-raising, or educational use.
For details, contact:
DK Publishing Special Markets, 1745 Broadway, 20th Floor, New York, NY 10019
SpecialSales@dk.com

Printed and bound in China
Super Readers Lexile® levels 620L to 790L
Lexile® is the registered trademark of MetaMetrics, Inc. Copyright © 2024 MetaMetrics, Inc. All rights reserved.

The publisher would like to thank the following for their kind permission to reproduce their images:
a=above; c=center; b=below; l=left; r=right; t=top; b/g=background
Alamy Stock Photo: Connect Images / Ghislain & Marie David de Lossy 45clb, Fairfax Media) / SuperStock / Frank Albert Charles
Burke / Sydney Morning Herald 22b, imageBROKER.com GmbH & Co. KG / Michael Weber 45tr, Moviestore Collection 45br, Science
History Images 28l, Shawshots 36-37t, True Images 35; **Dreamstime.com:** Yuri Arcurs 27, Ginasanders 44bl, Katarinagondova 22t,
Jannis Werner 29, Whitelander 44clb; **Getty Images:** Archive Photos / Buyenlarge 28b, Archive Photos / FPG / Staff 38, Archive
Photos / Ken Florey Suffrage Collection / Gado 36cra, Archive Photos / Museum of the City of New York 21, Bettmann 13, 33, 40, 43,
44cla, 45tl, Corbis Documentary / Brian Mitchell 9, Corbis Historical / Historical 30, 42cl, Fairfax Media 39, Moment Open / Brais Seara
16, The Image Bank / Wayne Eastep 24, Universal History Archive / Universal Images Group 32; **Getty Images / iStock:** Maksym
Belchenko 15, VacharapongW 20; **Penguin Random House LLC:** 31br; **Science Photo Library:** Library Of Congress 26b

Cover images: *Front:* **Dreamstime.com:** Sergey Lavrentev; **Getty Images:** Bettmann b;
Back: **Dreamstime.com:** Yehor Vlasenko cra, Ylivdesign cla, cl

www.dk.com

MIX
Paper | Supporting
responsible forestry
FSC™ C018179

This book was made with Forest
Stewardship Council™ certified
paper – one small step in DK's
commitment to a sustainable future.
**Learn more at www.dk.com/uk/
information/sustainability**

Helen Keller

Leslie Garrett & Matt Myers

Contents

Helen Keller visiting
with schoolchildren

Fever

Helen was a healthy baby. Her first year was filled with sights and sounds. She knew the faces of her mother and father. She had shiny toys. She heard birds singing. She saw sunlight streaming through the windows of her family's big house. She crawled around corners and under furniture.

But just as Helen was learning to walk, she got a very high fever. Doctors didn't think she would survive. But she did.

Helen Keller's childhood home. She was born in Tuscumbia, Alabama, on June 27, 1880.

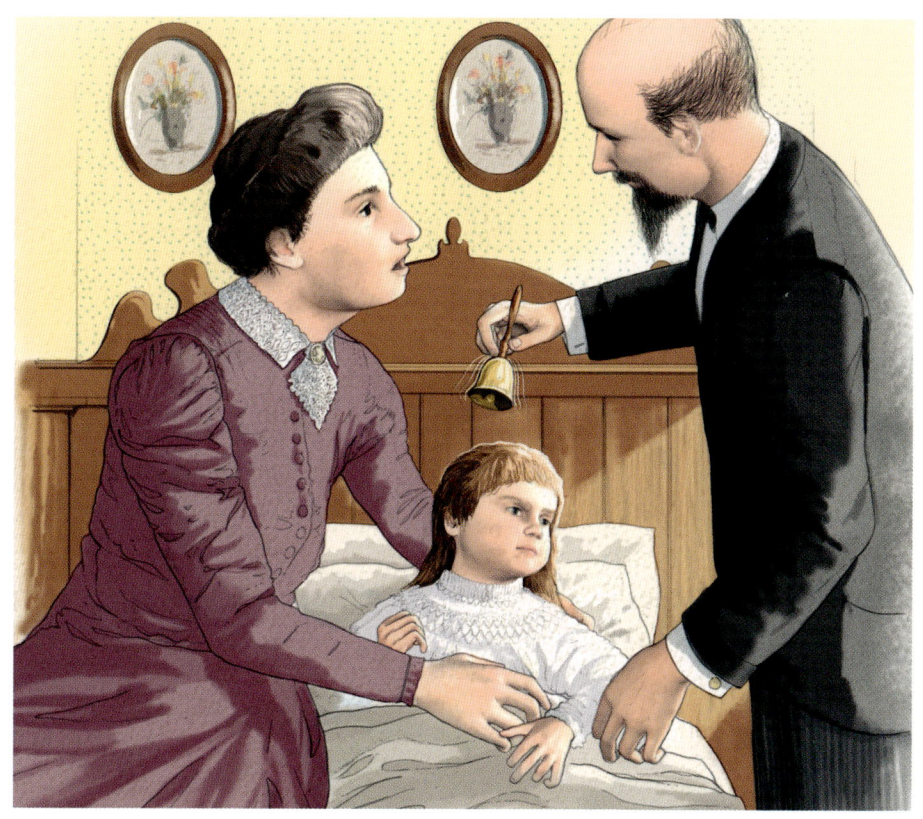

Over the next few days, however, Helen's parents noticed a change in her behavior. She didn't turn away from bright lights. She didn't respond to sounds.

The sickness had taken away Helen's sight and hearing. Suddenly, she was living in a dark, silent world. She would never again see her mother's face or hear her voice.

Helen was too young to understand what had happened. She felt lonely, scared, and angry at the world. Her parents didn't know what to do with their unhappy toddler.

Helen got bigger and stronger. Her behavior became difficult for her parents to handle.

The family welcomed a new baby. Helen didn't understand how delicate her sister was. Helen shoved the cradle over.

At that time, most kids with Helen's disabilities wouldn't have gotten any help. But the Kellers had enough money to hire someone to help. They met Alexander Graham Bell, who worked with deaf children. Bell was famous for inventing the telephone. He suggested that the family hire a special teacher just for Helen.

Yes, We Can
When Helen was a child, most people thought anyone who could not see or hear was less intelligent. They saw no point in trying to teach these people anything. Even today, people who are deafblind are sometimes treated as if they aren't smart enough to work, create, or teach. But they can do all these things and more.

The Stranger

The Kellers hired Anne Sullivan to be Helen's teacher. Anne had also been sick as a girl. She had lost most of her vision. But she'd had an operation on her eyes. It had given her enough sight to read.

Anne had recently graduated from the Perkins School for the Blind. She wanted to spend her life helping blind children. When she was picked to go help Helen, she was eager but worried. Helen wasn't just blind, but deaf, too. How would they be able to communicate?

Perkins School for the Blind

Perkins School for the Blind was in Boston, Massachusetts. The school's founder, Samuel Gridley Howe, taught a girl named Laura Bridgman. Like Helen, Laura had lost her sight and hearing after an illness as a young child. Laura was the first child with deafblindness known to be formally educated in the US. Her story was known throughout the world, decades before Helen was born.

The main building of Perkins, around 1893

Anne read everything she could find on how to reach people like Helen. Without sight or hearing, the answer had to be in the other three senses: touch, smell, and taste. Anne couldn't give lessons from a distance. She would need to touch Helen. She couldn't just be Helen's teacher. She would have to become her closest friend.

Helen was almost seven years old when she met Anne. Helen could tell something unusual was going to happen that day. Everyone was busy. She could smell things being cleaned. She could feel shoes thumping the floor. Her hair moved in the breezes of people rushing by her.

Someone approached Helen with light footsteps. Was it her mother? Helen came in for a hug, but the woman didn't feel right. Helen pulled away. This was not her mother. This was a stranger.

Helen with her dog, 1887

"Anne Sullivan," she told Helen's parents. "Call me Annie."

But of course, Helen couldn't hear Anne. She didn't even know what a name was.

Helen ignored Anne. She went back to life as she knew it. She was not a timid child. And when she found something she liked to do, she was happy.

She had even invented some hand signals that helped her communicate with her friend Martha. "We spent a great deal of time in the kitchen," Helen remembered years later. "Kneading dough balls, helping make ice-cream, grinding coffee, quarreling over the cake-bowl, and feeding the hens and turkeys that swarmed about the kitchen steps."

Eventually, Helen became curious about the new person in her house. She plunged her hands into Anne's suitcase. She used her sense of touch to identify objects. Anne had packed a doll, hoping Helen would explore. Helen felt the doll's tiny arms and legs. She moved her fingers over its face. Since she couldn't talk, she couldn't give the doll a name.

Anne reached gently for Helen's hand. She used her own hand to make letter shapes in Helen's palm. D-O-L-L, she spelled. Helen didn't understand. But she didn't pull away this time.

Anne's meals with the Keller family shocked her. Helen's parents allowed Helen to wander around the table. She took food from everyone's plate and crammed it into her mouth. And if Helen was upset, things got broken. She lashed out at anything in her way, including people. And Helen's parents did nothing.

Anne realized the Kellers had given up. They didn't know how to say no to a child who couldn't hear or see.

One day, Anne insisted that Helen sit in one place for a lesson. Helen was so angry, she knocked out one of Anne's teeth. Anne would never get anywhere with Helen in a house where she didn't need to behave. She asked the Kellers if she could take Helen somewhere else. Anne and Helen moved into a cottage on the Kellers' property.

The cottage where Anne and Helen lived

Finding Words

Helen was stubborn, but Anne was patient. She kept spelling words into Helen's hand. Helen quickly learned to make the same shapes with her own hands, but it was just a game to her. She even played the game with the family dog, her little fingers spelling into its paws.

Anne didn't know how to explain that letters represent sounds. When the sounds are put together, they create words. But what is a word? The word "water," for example, means nothing unless the mind can connect it to something.

Anne put Helen's hands under a stream of cold water. While the child was feeling it, Anne quickly spelled W–A–T–E–R into Helen's palm.

Suddenly, Helen understood. A door in her mind had swung open. She dropped to the ground, tugged on Anne's hand, and demanded to know what the world beneath them was called. D–I–R–T.

Set Free

Years later, Helen described her awakening. "The mystery of language was revealed to me. I knew then that W-A-T-E-R meant the wonderful cool something that was flowing over my hand. That living word awakened my soul, gave it light, hope, joy, set it free!"

Everything had a name! For the rest of the day, Helen led Anne everywhere, asking for the names of things. By the end of the day, she knew 30 words.

And it wasn't just Anne telling Helen things. Now Helen had a way to tell her teacher what was in her mind.

Helen fingerspelling into the hand of her friend Edith Thomas

Reading by Touch

It was time for the next step. Just before Helen turned eight, Anne gave her a big card with raised dots. The dots were a kind of writing called Braille. Braille letters were much faster to read than fingerspelling. By the end of the day, Helen had learned all the letters of this new alphabet.

There were whole books written in Braille. Soon, Helen was reading stories about distant places and times.

When Helen was reading, she was just like any other person. She had to picture the ideas in her mind. Helen was very good at that. She was used to relying on her imagination.

Helen reading around 1899

Braille
Braille is a form of written language that can be read with the fingertips. Braille was invented by a blind French boy named Louis Braille when he was just 15. This alphabet is represented by different combinations of six raised dots arranged in a grid. Through the use of Braille, Helen learned to read in five languages.

Becoming Famous

Some of Helen's early writing

Anne gave Helen a board with grooves in the shape of letters. By running a pencil along the grooves, Helen could write. It was just like making her own book!

As Helen learned more and more, she became famous. Newspapers ran stories about her. Famous people contacted her. She was even invited to meet President Grover Cleveland.

Helen feels Anne's lips while using fingerspelling to communicate with Alexander Graham Bell, 1894.

What Is Speech?
Many people, including Bell, used to think people who were deaf could only be part of society if they learned to talk out loud. Today, sign languages are considered speaking, just like any other language. There are more than 300 sign languages in the world.

Helen also spent time with Alexander Graham Bell. Though he is remembered for the telephone, his life's work was dedicated to working with people who were deaf. He wanted to enable them to talk not just with their hands, but also with their voices.

Helen wanted to try. When she was nine, she got help from Sarah Fuller, a school principal. Helen touched Fuller's mouth. While Fuller spoke, Helen felt the exact positions of Fuller's tongue and lips when she made each sound. Helen imitated her motions and produced the same sounds. Helen would never speak very clearly, but now she had another way to express herself.

Keller and Twain, around 1901

In 1895, when Helen was 14, she met Mark Twain, a famous American author. Although he was much older than she, Helen and Twain quickly became friends. They loved animals. They were both funny. Best of all, Twain accepted her as an equal, someone to share ideas with.

Samuel Clemens

Mark Twain was the pen name for a writer named Samuel Clemens. He is best known for his fictional characters Tom Sawyer and Huckleberry Finn. But Twain also spoke out against war and corporate greed, as Helen Keller would come to do.

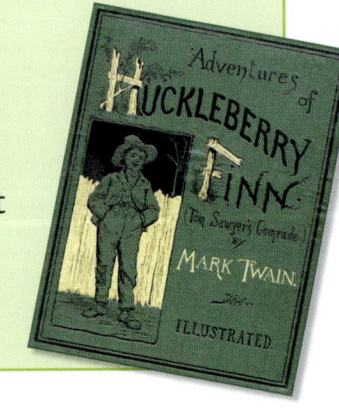

Twain encouraged Helen to keep writing. She had already published a story. He believed Helen could become whatever she wanted to be. He raised money for her to go to college. When Helen was 16, she entered a school that would prepare her for college.

But not everyone believed in Helen. They warned her that no deafblind person had ever gone to college. They advised her not to try what no one else had tried before. She was foolish, they said, and sure to fail. Helen didn't listen.

Radcliffe College

A Graduate and an Author

College was much harder for Helen than for other students. None of the textbooks were in Braille. Other students listened to lessons and took notes. Anne Sullivan had to sit next to Helen, finger-spelling as fast as she could. Sullivan read textbooks, also through finger writing, to Helen for four or five hours a day. Helen had to memorize everything.

At Radcliffe, teachers were impressed by Helen's intellect and determination. They encouraged her to write her life story. Helen was only 22, but what a life she had already had!

She wrote the book. And she graduated from college with honors. At the graduation ceremony, the audience gave her a standing ovation. She was the first person with deafblindness to earn a college degree.

Early Life Story

Keller's memoir, *The Story of My Life*, was published in 1903. It became an international bestseller. She would go on to write many more books.

the
story
of
my
Life
Helen Keller

With an Afterword by Marlee Matlin

Children at work in a US glass factory, 1908

An Ugly World

As the world opened up to Keller, she understood that it wasn't all wonderful. Cruelty and injustice were everywhere. Poor children worked in factories. Those with disabilities were treated as incomplete people. Women could not vote or go to any college they wanted. Radcliffe was where women went instead of Harvard, where only men were accepted. And while Radcliffe had just started to admit Black students, most colleges did not.

Keller was amazed that people could be so "boneheaded." Their eyes and ears worked. Could they not see the injustice? Could they not hear the suffering? Some people spoke out against the cruelty, including Keller's friends Mark Twain and W. E. B. Du Bois. But more voices were needed.

Keller had already accomplished so much. But now she realized her life's work had just begun.

W. E. B. Du Bois
W. E. B. Du Bois was the first Black person to earn a PhD from Harvard University. He co-founded the National Association for the Advancement of Colored People (NAACP) to help Black people get justice. He and Keller met often in New York to discuss politics.

Helen Keller Speaks Out

With Sullivan's help, Keller gave speeches to huge crowds. She was very popular, especially when she repeated stories of her childhood. But she was a grown woman now. She wanted to talk about other things, too.

Why did America spend money on war and take over other countries? Keller thought it was obvious that the money should be used to fix problems at home. America had plenty of problems. Poverty. Racism. The way women were treated. In her book *Out of the Dark*, Keller described her growing world view.

Sullivan and Keller

Keller asked audiences why American women were not allowed to vote. She had proved what a woman was capable of, even in extremely challenging circumstances. Being a woman, Keller declared, held her back more than any of her disabilities.

The Perkins Brailler, a Braille typewriter

Many newspapers considered Keller's ideas too negative. People stopped attending her speeches. Who was this new Helen Keller? They seemed to like her better when all she could say was W–A–T–E–R.

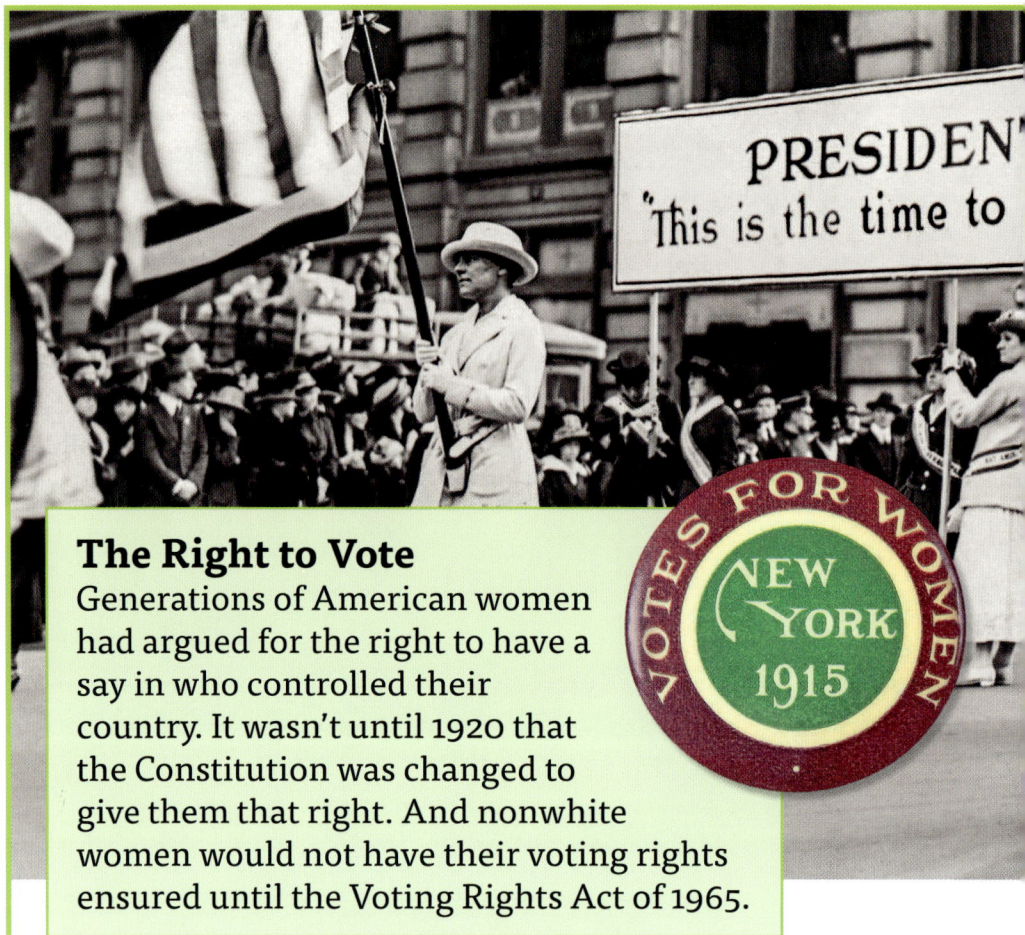

The Right to Vote
Generations of American women had argued for the right to have a say in who controlled their country. It wasn't until 1920 that the Constitution was changed to give them that right. And nonwhite women would not have their voting rights ensured until the Voting Rights Act of 1965.

Keller didn't care about being popular. She joined protest marches with other women, demanding the right to vote.

She blamed rich and powerful people for oppressing poor people. "Money talks so loud," she said, "that the voice of the people is drowned." She fought for better wages and safer working conditions.

ILSON SAYS :
ort Woman Suffrage."

PRES_____NT WILS_
'I urge the peo____ew York to set a
for Woman Suffra___sk you to convey

US women's suffrage march, 1915

She joined the American Socialist Party in 1908. She supported a form of government that distributes wealth equally among its citizens.

Many people didn't want to believe Keller thought this way. *Life* magazine claimed that other people were telling her what to think and say. But Keller's opinions were her own.

Keller accused the US of being racist. She wrote a letter of support for the NAACP. It said, "This great republic of ours is a mockery when citizens in any section are denied the rights which the Constitution guarantees them."

Keller warned people about German Chancellor Adolf Hitler before most Americans even knew who he was. She condemned his treatment of Jewish people in 1933, more than 10 years before his campaign of mass murder was finally stopped.

She spoke out against all wars. She urged people not to fight. She urged workers not to make weapons of war. Many people thought this kind of talk was un-American.

But Keller supported American soldiers. She visited the wounded, many of whom had been blinded in combat.

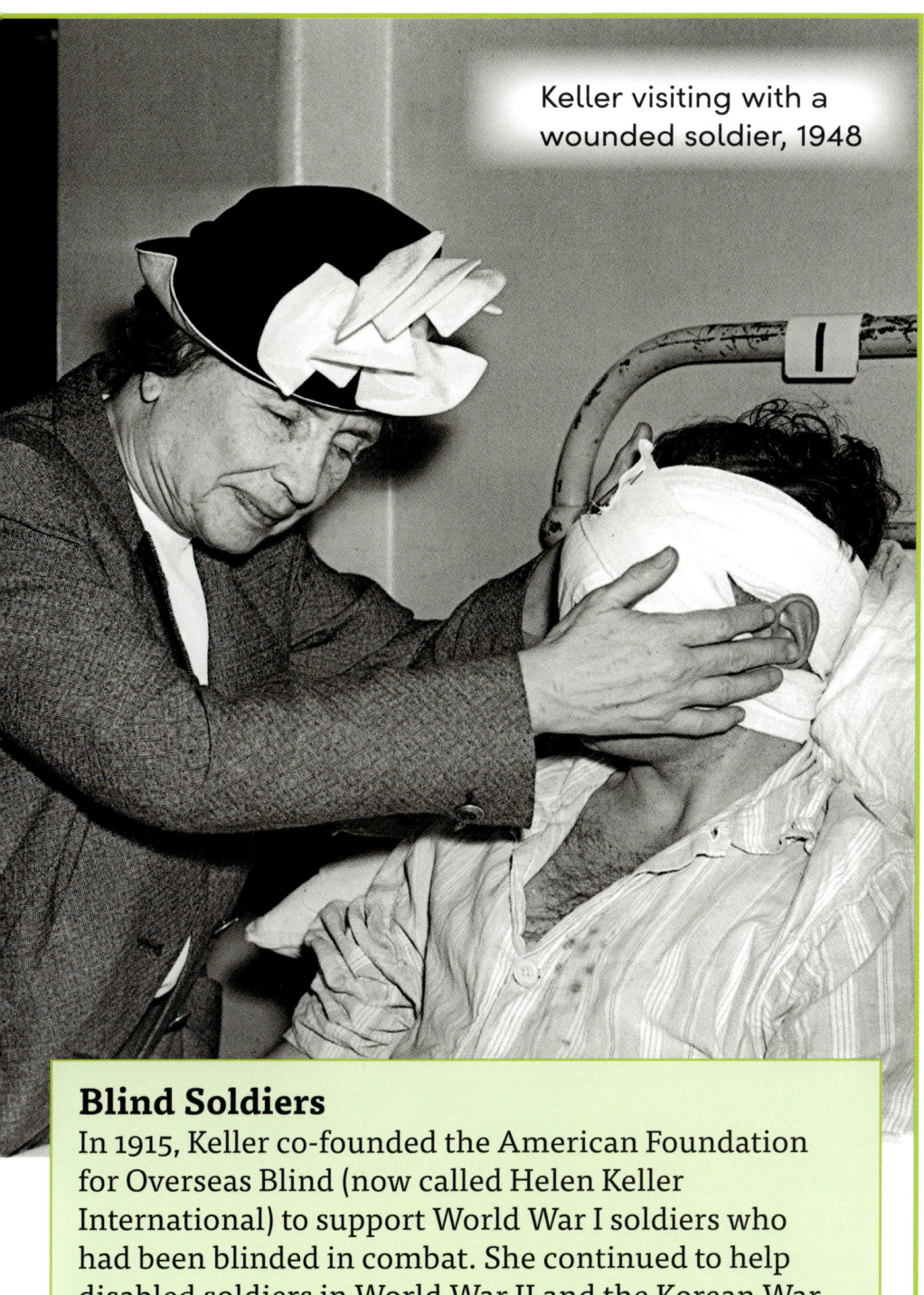

Keller visiting with a wounded soldier, 1948

Blind Soldiers

In 1915, Keller co-founded the American Foundation for Overseas Blind (now called Helen Keller International) to support World War I soldiers who had been blinded in combat. She continued to help disabled soldiers in World War II and the Korean War.

Left to right: Charlie Chaplin, Polly Thomson, Helen Keller, and Anne Sullivan, 1918

Personal Life

Keller had close friendships with famous people such as film star Charlie Chaplin and First Lady Eleanor Roosevelt. But her dearest friends were Anne Sullivan, and then the woman became her interpreter after Sullivan's death, Polly Thomson.

Thomson started as Keller's assistant, but soon became her interpreter and close friend. For 46 years, Thomson traveled everywhere with Keller, often acting as her bodyguard when people got too close.

Peter Fagan worked for Keller as an interpreter. The two enjoyed long walks in the woods. They shared thoughts on politics and spirituality. They fell in love and planned to marry. But Keller's family were against it. They put so much pressure on the couple that they broke off their engagement. It was a loss Keller would mourn for the rest of her life.

Quiet Happiness

Keller continued to support humanitarian causes for the rest of her life. She toured the world into her 70s, sharing her thoughts. When Keller finally did retire, she had more time for the simple things she enjoyed as a child. She had bought a house in the country, with a big garden and lots of dogs. As Keller once said, "When one door of happiness closes, another opens."

Sir Thomas, one of Keller's many dogs

Always a Child

Keller has been portrayed in many books and films, most famously in *The Miracle Worker*. Yet most stories about her life end just as she is learning to communicate, before she became a woman with so much to say.

The film *Helen Keller in Her Story*, also called *The Unconquered,* won the Oscar for best documentary feature film of 1955. Keller holds the award statue in 1956.

1882
Keller loses her sight and hearing.

1903
Keller's first book, *The Story of My Life,* is published.

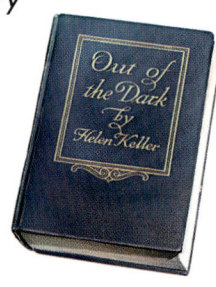

1913
Keller's book *Out of the Dark* challenges society to overcome its own lack of awareness.

1887
Anne Sullivan begins teaching Keller.

1920
Keller co-founds the American Civil Liberties Union.

1880   **1900**   **1920**

1919
1919 Keller stars in *Deliverance*, a film about her life.

1880
Helen Keller is born.

1904
Keller graduates cum laude from Radcliffe College.

1946–1957
Keller tours 35 countries, promoting awareness about blindness.

1968
Keller dies.

1973
Keller is inducted into the National Women's Hall of Fame.

1952
Keller is honored by the National Institute of Social Sciences for service to humanity.

1940　　　　　**1960**　　　　　**1980**

1964
Keller is awarded the Presidential Medal of Freedom.

1933
Keller's books are burned by Adolf Hitler's Nazi party.

1962
The Miracle Worker, a film about Keller's childhood, wins many awards.

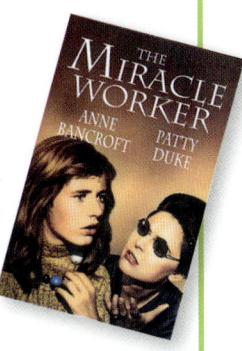

Glossary

Blind
Unable to see

Braille
A system of writing that uses patterns of raised dots that can be felt with the fingertips

Capable
Able to do things

College
A school where people study specific subjects at a high level

Combat
Fighting during a war

Cottage
A small house

Deaf
Unable to hear

Deafblind
Unable to hear or to see

Disability
A condition that interferes with a person's ability to do certain things

Engagement
An agreement to be married

Fever
A very high body temperature caused by disease or infection

Graduate
To complete one's education at a particular school

Humanitarian
Related to improving people's quality of life

Imitate
To do something the way another person does it

Injustice
Unfair treatment

Interpreter
A person who translates words from one language to another

NAACP
The National Association for the Advancement of Colored People, an organization founded in 1909 to demand equality and fight injustice

Poverty
The condition of not having enough money to live comfortably

Protest
To express pain, unhappiness, or dissatisfaction about a situation

Racism
Unfair treatment because of one's skin color or race

Sign language
A language spoken through hand positions and gestures

Socialist
Relating to a form of government that tries to make things fair for all its citizens

Index

Quiz

Answer the questions to see what you have learned. Check your answers in the key below.

1. True or false: Helen Keller was born deafblind.

2. How old was Helen when Anne Sullivan came to work with her?

3. What was the title of Keller's first published book?

4. Keller worked to help get women the right to _____.

5. What organization did Keller co-found to help war veterans who had been blinded in combat?

1. False 2. Seven 3. *The Story of My Life* 4. Vote 5. American Foundation for Overseas Blind (or Helen Keller International)